THE POWER OF A POSITIVIST

ANU AGRAWAL

Contents

1.

"Hard work, prayers and dedication towards the right path is the panacea for your deplorable state."

2.

Prolific success gives a lot of happiness, divine peace and complete satisfaction.

3.

""An invincible personality appears jokey to all."

4.

"Give your damnedest to your tasks

and

then see the miracles that occurs in your life."

5.

An incipient always reaches towards his/her goal if he/she has a positive mindset and a judicious attitude.

6.

A self-lover, motivator and an optimist who is directed towards his/her dream is a dynamo.

7.

Pray to God in your predicament

and say to yourself

"this too shall pass."

8.

Give respect take respect.

Give nonsense take nonsense.

9.

Earn your spectator's happiness

and confidence through

your wonderful performance.

10.

Always make your talk succinct so

that it does not bore your spectators.

11.

Enunciate your success and

work hard and smart to achieve it.

12.

A person must have a magnetic

and a fascinating personality.

13.

Keep on ignoring things and

people to protect your peace.

14.

Subdue your weakness,

your fears, your

bad habits and

your negative thinking.

15.

Accrue your knowledge in

the field that interests you.

16.

Gratify your inner strengths and

then you will be unstoppable.

17.

Beset yourself with successful people

and you will be one of them.

18.

SUCCESS=SATISFACTION

WEALTH=FREEDOM

19.

Every trouble goes

and

the dawn arrives.

20.

If your intuition tells that it is right then it is right and if your intuition tells that it is wrong then it is wrong.

21.

Dissipate your fears and do all the things that you want to do.

22.

Maintain your composure when you reach at the highest level of your life.

23.

Your health, character, wealth and relationships are your prerequisites.

24.

Your rival is your best companion.

25.

.Always be elated whether people like it or not.

26.

Subtle minds are often creative ones.

27.

Vow yourself that you are going to achieve all that you want in your life.

28.

Don't be a milquetoast rather be a fearless icon.

29.

Healthy food is our basic need.
Consuming salads and
fruits are our strength
and consuming junk foods
is our weakness.

30.

Be proactive for your fitness
and make healthy nutrition
your first priority.

31.

Be covetous for your success
and it will come to
you infinitely.

32.

Remove all impediments from
your life and focus on
your expansion and growth.

33.

Birthdays are always special.
It has nothing to do with age.

34.

Capitulate yourself in superior
books and then finally grow
and expand in your life.

35.

Ample amount of knowledge
of your work is necessary
to attain success.

36.

A diplomatic person is

loved and respected by all.

37.

Incredible is your thinking

Incredible are your actions

Incredible is your accomplishment

Incredible is your journey.

38.

Optimum utilization of resources

is essential to get achievement.

39.

Practice for your infallible performance

and you will certainly win the world.

40.

Assimilate thoughts of superiority,

goodness, peace and abundance.

41.

Let's aliment our beautiful mind

with great thoughts of abundance.

42.

Caring comes from our precious

hearts as we can feel the

love for another person inside us.

43.

Expressions on your face

speaks a lot about

your personality.

44.

Understanding between

two people comes

through communication.

45.

Naivety is always appreciated,

remembered and accepted.

46.

Music according to your

mood makes you feel better.

47.

Success is extreme happiness

that comes from within.

48.

Your health is your biggest

treasure so decide how

you are going to maintain it.

49.

Muster all your courage to

fight for what you truly want.

50.

If you really want to enjoy

your life then you must go

on a beach.

51.

You can mold your body

by doing gym but you

can mold your mind

by doing meditation.

52.

Heal yourself by repeating positive statements again and again.

53.

An experience in our life is necessary whether it is good or bad.

54.

Babies are innocent flowers.

55.

Your subconscious mind only accepts what your conscious mind constantly gives.

56.

Make vivid images in your mind of what you want in your life.

57.

Life is like a rainbow.
Each and every color has its own importance.

58.

Daily reading is best habit.

59.

Exercising daily will give you physical success and good health.

60.

Natural talent in a person is god gifted.
Make the best possible use of it.

61.

Relationships must be
protracted and based
on love, trust,
confidence and respect.

62.

Naturality should
always be preserved.

63.

The Law of Universe is always
helping you to achieve your goals.

64.

Send beautiful thoughts to your
subconscious mind and
achieve excellent results in your life.

65.

Praying to God is one of
the best way to relax
your holy heart and
calm your wonderful mind.

66.

Begin your beautiful day with
a smile on your cute face
and happiness in your generous heart.

67.

Beautiful habits equal
to favorable outcomes.

68.

Eat healthy. Live healthy.
Think healthy.

Be the janitor of your health.

69.

Suggestions of terror made to

a person full of conviction

and trust have absolutely no effect.

70.

Vitriolic fights should be avoided.

71.

An innocent person must stop

suffering at the hands of others actions.

72.

Always stay persistent and consistent.

73.

Expunge bad memories from

your mind and supplant

it with good ones.

74.

Sometimes the awkward moments

teach you the bestest lesson of your life.

75.

Avoid feeling of retaliation as it is not good.

76.

Inconsequential topics should

not be a part of discussion.

77.

Physical beauty of a woman

can be defined but her

inner beauty is indefinable.

78.

Prognosticators are the ones

who leaves us in dilemma.

Believe in yourself.

79.

Elucidate your talk and

always speak straight

to the point.

80.

Replace your fast food

with fruit and you'll have

less of craving to snacks,

and more nourishment

in your system.

81.

Be aware of your daily

routine in order to detect

harmful habits and supplant

them with more optimistic ones.

82.

Those who face challenges with

a good attitude and are able

to manage their sentiments

are already efficient on

their route toward long-life.

83.

Frame of mind can help break

negative cycles and decrease worry.

84.

Too-much attention to

a desire can keep that desire
from being accomplished.

85.

Generate new emotions on
the foundation of actions.

86.

In sentiments, it is best to
be rich and magnanimous.

87.

Eat in a balanced way, do
low-light exercise, and
learn not to surrender
when trouble arise.

88.

If you are offended and
want to combat, think about
it for two days before coming to blast.
After two days the extreme
desire to combat will pass on its own.

89.

Add a small something additional,
something that takes you out of your cozy zone.

90.

As soon as you take the
first small step, your worry
will vanish and you will
gain a sweet flow in the
activity you're doing.

91.

Focusing on single thing at
a time can be the only
most prime factor in attaining flow.

92.

Can an individual actually retire
if he is affectionate regarding what he does?

93.

Our capability to tum regular
tasks into moments of microflow,
into something we derive
pleasure is key to our being glad.

94.

Experts know how crucial
it is to safeguard their space,
control their surroundings,
and be unoccupied of disturbances.

95.

Educating the mind can get
us to a place of flow more promptly.

96.

Meditation is one way to
keep-fit our intellectual power.

97.

The most significant thing is
to concentrate on the path of life.

98.

To live for many years, you need to do four things:
i. Workout to stay fit
ii. Eat healthy

iii. Keep smiling

iv. Spend time with your love ones.

99.

Conversing every single day
with your loved ones, that's
the secret to longevity.

100.

Doing various things daily.
Consistently staying occupied,
but doing single thing at a time,
without getting overwhelmed.

101.

Daily I say to myself,
"Today will be full
of strength and enthusiasm.
Live it to the max."

102.

If we want to get improved at
reaching a state of flow,
meditation is an outstanding remedy
to our smartphones and their notifications
continuously screaming for our attention.

103.

A great fortitude inside a person
will definitely lead him/her towards victory.

104.

Yoga aspires to connect body
and mind in the same way,
leading us toward an active

lifestyle in unity with the world around us.

105.

The main goals of yoga are:

i. To bring us near to humanity

ii. Physical and mental satisfaction

iii. To bring us closer to the almighty.

106.

Perfect exercising for our mind,

body and emotional resilience

is vital for facing life's highs and lows.

107.

There is nothing bad with

celebrating life's luxuries as

long as they do not take

power of your life as you

cherish them.

108.

Brooding about things

that are beyond our control

achieves nothing.

We should have a clear idea

of what we can change and what we can't,

which in turn will permit us to

prevent giving in to weak emotions.

109.

In place of seeking for beauty in perfection,

we should gaze for it in

things that are faulty, imperfect.

110.

Only things that are flawed,
imperfect and momentary can exactly
be beautiful because only such
things resemble the pure world.

111.

Be led by your interest,
and keep occupied by
doing things that fill you
with meaning and gladness.

112.

Life is not an issue to be figured out.
Just be sure to have something that
keeps you occupied doing what you love
while being circled by the people who love you.

113.

Cease mourning the past and panicking
about the future. Today is all you have.
Make the most of it.
Make it worth looking back.

114.

Everybody seems to have a
complete idea of how other
humans should lead their
lives, but nobody about his or her own.

115.

The Spirit of the Universe is
cherished by people's cheerfulness.

116.

To understand one's fortune

is a person's only actual duty.

117.

Alchemists are curious people,
who think only about themselves,
and almost every time
declined to help others.

118.

Every blessing disregarded
tum out to be a malediction.

119.

When you desire something,
all the world cooperates
in supporting you to accomplish it.

120.

The nearer one gets to understanding
his fortune, the more that fortune
becomes his faithful reason for living.

121.

Humans need not fear the unrevealed
if they are efficient of attaining
what they require and want.

122.

Jewel is discovered by the power
of running water, and it is
hidden by the same currents.

123.

Alchemy is a solemn determination.

124.

Everybody has his or her

personal way of studying things.

125.

It's only those who are determined,
and ready to learn things passionately,
who attain the crowning achievement.

126.

Everything on earth is being incessantly
enhanced because the earth is breathing....
And it has a feeling.

127.

Making a choice was only
the starting of things.

128.

Boldness is an attribute most
crucial to understanding the
accent of the world.

129.

When something is penned,
there is no way to alter it.

130.

If what one obtains is made of
authentic stuff, it will never tarnish.

131.

"We are scared of losing what
we have, whether it's our life
or our belongings and assets.
But this terror disappears when
we realize that our life tales
and the history of the

world were penned by the same hand."

132.

The presence of this world is
clearly a proof that there resides
a world that is flawless.

133.

Every hunt starts with learner's fortune.
And every hunt finishes
with the winner's being critically experimented.

134.

When you own immense valuables
inside you, and make an effort to
say others of them, seldom are you trusted.

135.

When we aspire to become finer
than we are, all the things around
us becomes finer, too.

136.

A student is self-described and
self-driven, constantly trying to
enhance his understanding so that he
can move on to the next subject,
the next challenge. A real student is
also his own tutor and his own
evaluator. There is no space for ego there.

137.

Opportunities are not usually profound,
virgin pools that need fortitude and
forwardness to jump into, but instead

are concealed, dotted over,
jammed by several forms of resistance.

138.

Aim is about chasing something
outside yourself as contradicted to
entertaining yourself.

139.

The crucial work that you want
to do will need your consultation
and attention. Not zeal. Not innocence.

140.

Excellence comes from polite
initiations; it comes from thankless task.
It means you're the insignificant
person in the room-until you
change that with outcomes.

141.

Our own route, whatever we desire to,
will in some ways be described by
the quantity of foolishness we are
ready to handle.

142.

It doesn't matter how brilliant you are,
how excellent your links are,
how much wealth you have.
When you desire to do
something-something great and
significant and useful you will be

assigned to treatment ranging
from ordinariness to complete destruction.
Count on it.

143.

Ego is an immoral act because
it is a lie-it persuades people
that they are superior than they are,
that they are superior than Almighty
made them. Ego leads to aloofness and
then away from humility and
association with their companion.

144.

Effort is finding yourself lonely at
the track when the climate kept
everybody else within doors.

145.

A tyro is aggressive.
The experienced finds learning
to be delightful, they like being
questioned and unpretending ,
and absorb in education as
continuing and perpetual process.

146.

As people grow, they must also
perceive how they observe and
then set up procedures to
promote this incessant education.

147.

Truth is worthier than

story and picture.

148.

All of us misspend valuable life
doing things we don't like,
to show ourselves to people
we don't honor, and to get
things we don't want.

149.

Each one of us has a special capability
and aim, that indicates that we're the
only ones who can figure out and
set the terms of our lives.

150.

Make it about the effort and the
ideas behind it-not about a
splendid imagination that
makes a better headline.

151.

Wealth means defeating the
bazaar and the probabilities.

152.

An intelligent man or woman
must consistently remind themselves
of the boundaries of their potential and reach.

153.

Victory involved neglecting the
suspicions and restrictions of the
people near us. It meant refusing
rejection. It needed taking definite risks.

154.

As you become victorious in your own field, your duties may start to change. Days become less and less about executing and more and more about making choices. Such is the description of captainship.

155.

Every idea and target demand an outlook suited flawlessly to what needs to be done. Maybe an innovative, carefree environment makes the most sense for what you're carrying out.

156.

Ego requires reverences in order to be approved. Conviction, on the other hand, is capable to wait and concentrate on the piece of work regardless of outer recognition.

157.

By eliminating the ego-even momentarily-we can access what's left standing in relief. By enlarging our viewpoint, more comes into view.

158.

Don't be deluded by recognition you have obtained or the great deal of money in your bank account.

159.

Too-much attention to a desire can
keep that desire from being accomplished.

160.

Travelling is the best thing to remove
all the worries that are there in
our lives and also we get rid
of our daily routine.

161.

Books are our friends and enemies.
If we choose to read the right book
then it proves to be our friend but if we
choose to read an incorrect book
then it destroys our one and only mind.

162.

If your fame can't digest a few blows,
it wasn't deserving anything in the initial place.

163.

Most problem is short-term....
except you make that not so.
Comeback is not grand, it's one
pace ahead of the other.
Except your cure is more of the illness.

164.

The society can show you the fact,
but no one can compel you to admit it.

165.

Success is calmness of mind,
which is a straight outcome of

self-satisfaction in knowing
you made the effort to do your
best to turn out to be the best
that you are efficient of becoming.

166.

All successful men and women
went through adversities to get to
where they are, all of them made errors.
They found within those adventures some
advantage-even if it was simply the awareness
that they were not perfect and that things would not
always go their way. They found that self-examination
was the way out and through-if they hadn't, they
wouldn't have gotten stronger and they
wouldn't have been able to stand up again.

167.

It is great to honor the guru.
Gain information from him.
Pay attention to him.
Study him. But don't worship him.
Trust you can be better than him.
Trust you can go ahead.
Those who cherish the second-best
attitude are always second-best achievers.

168.

Think great and you'll live great.
You'll live great in cheerfulness.
You'll live great in triumph.
Great in earnings.

Great in buddies, Great in respect.

Printed by Libri Plureos GmbH in Hamburg,
Germany